The Story of Esther

By Patricia A. Pingry
Illustrated by Susan J. Harrison

IDEALS CHILDREN'S BOOKS
Nashville, Tennessee

Copyright © 1989 by Ideals Publishing Corporation
All rights reserved.
Printed and bound in the United States of America.
Published by Ideals Publishing Corporation
Nashville, Tennessee
ISBN 0-8249-8420-X

For my mother

— S. J. H.

A Word to Parents and Friends

This story is one of a series of biblical stories especially written, illustrated, and designed to explain a difficult concept in a gentle and simple manner.

Even the youngest child will understand the timeless lesson inherent in each bible story. Most of all, preschoolers, beginning readers, and older children will enjoy hearing and reading these accounts of heroes from one of the oldest and most exciting books of all: the Holy Bible.

Far away and long ago, an announcement swept throughout the ancient land of Persia. King Xerxes was searching for the most meek and most beautiful woman in the land to be his queen.

In the country lived a kind and gentle girl named Esther. Her cousin Mordecai brought Esther before the king. The king took one look at her and chose her as his queen.

Mordecai often sat outside the king's gates listening to the gossip. One day he overheard two guards plotting to kill the king.

Mordecai told Esther, who in turn told the king. King Xerxes then had the men arrested and hanged.

One day, one of the king's officers, a man named Haman, was honored by the king. Everyone at the king's gate knelt down to Haman. All but Mordecai. Mordecai was a Jew and bowed to no one but God.

Haman knew Mordecai the Jew; and when he saw Mordecai refuse to kneel, he grew very angry. He vowed to kill Mordecai. Haman was so angry he vowed to kill all the Jews. He needed only to name the day. To do so, Haman and his soldiers cast lots, called *Pur*.

Haman then had to tell the king what *he* had decided. He said, "Did you know there are people in your kingdom who defy the customs and laws of the land? It would be best to put these people to death."

With this lie, Haman obtained the king's permission to have the Jews put to death.

The word went out that the Jews were to be killed in the month of *Adar*. Mordecai wailed and wept. He and all the Jews tore their clothes and dressed in sackcloth, the custom of mourning. Esther had not heard of the king's decree; and when her maids told her about Mordecai, Esther sent him food and clothing.

But Mordecai sent this reply to Esther: "Don't think that you will be spared just because you live in the palace. When the king discovers that you are a Jew, he will kill you too. Who knows? Maybe God made you queen just for this moment."

Esther didn't like to hear that! What can I do? she said to herself. The king sometimes kills those who come before him without being summoned.

Finally, Esther sent word to Mordecai: "Gather all the Jews in the city. Pray and do not eat for three days and nights. Then I will go to the king."

After three days, Esther put on her royal robes and crown and entered the king's chambers.

"What do you want, Esther?" King Xerxes asked.

Esther was frightened, but she stood up and said, "I most humbly request the presence of your majesty and your servant Haman at a banquet I have prepared."

The king could not refuse such a humble request.

So the king and Haman went to the banquet, and they ate and drank and watched the entertainment Esther provided. At the end of this, King Xerxes asked once more, "Esther, what is it that you wish?"

Esther meekly replied, "I most humbly request the presence of your majesty and your servant Haman at a banquet I have prepared for tomorrow. Then I will tell you what I desire."

Of course, all this made Haman very proud. He thought he was a very important man indeed.

Haman went home and told his wife, "I am the only one Queen Esther invited to be with the king. And the king and I return tomorrow for another banquet! If only I didn't have to see that wretched Mordecai every time I enter the king's gate."

Haman's wife suggested to him, "Have a gallows built today. In the morning, you can ask the king to hang Mordecai on it. I'm sure the king will do whatever you ask. Then you can go to the banquet a happy man." So Haman had the gallows built.

That night the king could not sleep, so he read the history of his reign. He read of Mordecai's exposure of the plot to kill him. In the morning, he asked his attendants, "Did I honor Mordecai for saving my life?"

"No my king," came the answer.

Just then, Haman came to ask the king to hang Mordecai.

But before Haman could speak, the king asked, "What is a good way to honor a man?"

Haman thought, He is going to honor *me*. So he said, "Place the king's robe on the man's shoulders and his crown upon his head. Place him on the king's horse and have a prince lead him through the streets shouting, 'This is a man the king thinks highly of'."

"Then go," said the king. "Get the robe, the crown, and the horse and do as you have suggested to Mordecai the Jew." So Haman did as the king commanded.

Haman was humiliated. He wanted to go home and hide. Instead, he had to go to the banquet prepared by Esther for the king.

After the banquet was over, King Xerxes again asked Esther, "What can I do for you? Up to half my kingdom is yours if you but ask."

Esther responded, "If it pleases you, grant me my life and spare my people, for we are to be killed."

"Who would do such a thing?" asked the king.

"The wicked Haman!" replied Esther.

Haman was so terrified that he thought he would faint. King Xerxes leaped to his feet and shouted for his guards. One of the soldiers said, "There is a gallows outside Haman's house."

"Hang him on that!" shouted the king.

So Queen Esther saved her people and reigned for many years. Mordecai moved to the castle as the king's most trusted adviser. And the Jews live on, even to the present day.